the CREATION story for children

Written by
Helen Haidle

Illustrated by
David Haidle
Cheri Bladholm

First printing: July 2009

ISBN-13: 978-0-89051-565-5
ISBN-10: 0-89051-565-4
Library of Congress: 00033385

Unless otherwise noted, all Scripture is from the King James Version of the Bible.

Printed in China.

Please visit our website for other great titles:
www.masterbooks.net.

For information regarding author interviews, please contact the publicity department at (870) 438-5288.

Genesis 1:1–2 KJV

"In the beginning God created the heaven and the earth.
And the earth was without form, and void; and darkness was upon the face of the deep. And the Spirit of God moved upon the face of the waters."

Try to imagine what it must have been like before God made the world.

Nothing else existed, except God.

WHO is God? The Almighty, All-knowing and All-powerful One who made everything we know and see.

In the beginning, this God—the giver of all life—now began to work in the darkness.

Genesis 1:3–5

"And God said, Let there be light: and there was light. And God saw the light, that it was good: and God divided the light from the darkness. And God called the light Day, and the darkness he called Night. And the evening and the morning were the first day."

The Bible tells us, "God is light." Would you rather live in the darkness or in the light? What could you see or do if everything was dark?

Just like God saw that the light was good, all of us know light is a very good thing. Look at all the beautiful rainbow colors that are in LIGHT.

Genesis 1:6-8

"And God said, Let there be a firmament in the midst of the waters, and let it divide the waters from the waters.

And God made the firmament, and divided the waters which were under the firmament from the waters which were above the firmament: and it was so.

And God called the firmament Heaven. And the evening and the morning were the second day."

What do you see overhead in God's big sky? Clouds are formed when billions of water droplets come together.

Water fills up the clouds and then falls to the earth as rain or snow.

Next time you go outside, look up and thank God for sky and clouds.

Genesis 1:9–10

"And God said, Let the waters under the heaven be gathered together unto one place, and let the dry land appear: and it was so.

And God called the dry land Earth; and the gathering together of the waters called he Seas: and God saw that it was good."

Water is so important. No plant or animal or person can live without water. Our bodies need water to drink even more than we need food to eat.

Do you enjoy water? Do you ever swim in a lake, watch a waterfall, or walk on a beach as the waves roll on shore?

God said all the water is "GOOD!" Oh, yes! We can't live without it.

Genesis 1:11–13

"And God said, Let the earth bring forth grass, the herb yielding seed, and the fruit tree yielding fruit after his kind, whose seed is in itself, upon the earth: and it was so...
And God saw that it was good.
And the evening and the morning were the third day."

God gave us many different kinds of plants. Flowers and trees make our world beautiful. Fruits and vegetables help our bodies grow strong.

And every plant produces a special "seed" that grows into a new plant.

How many of these plants do you eat? Aren't you glad they taste good?

11

Genesis 1:14, 16, 18–19

"God said, Let there be lights in the firmament of the heaven to divide the day from the night; and let them be for signs, and for seasons, and for days, and years...
And God made two great lights...to rule the day, and...to rule the night...and God saw that it was good.
And the evening and the morning were the fourth day."

The sun, moon, and billions of stars show us how strong and mighty God is. Even with the most powerful telescope, no one finds the "end" of the universe.

Go outside tonight and look up in the sky. Shining planets and stars give God glory as they whirl through space.

Genesis 1:20–22

"And God said, Let the waters bring forth abundantly the moving creature that hath life...

And God created great whales, and every living creature that moveth, which the waters brought forth abundantly, after their kind...God saw that it was good.

God blessed them, saying, Be fruitful, and multiply, and fill the waters in the seas..."

God made so many sea creatures—from the great whale to the tiny diatom (*see top row*). Look at all their interesting shapes and colors.

Can you find the different fins and tails that help fish swim?

Some sea creatures live in a shell. Some look like stars. Which are your favorites?

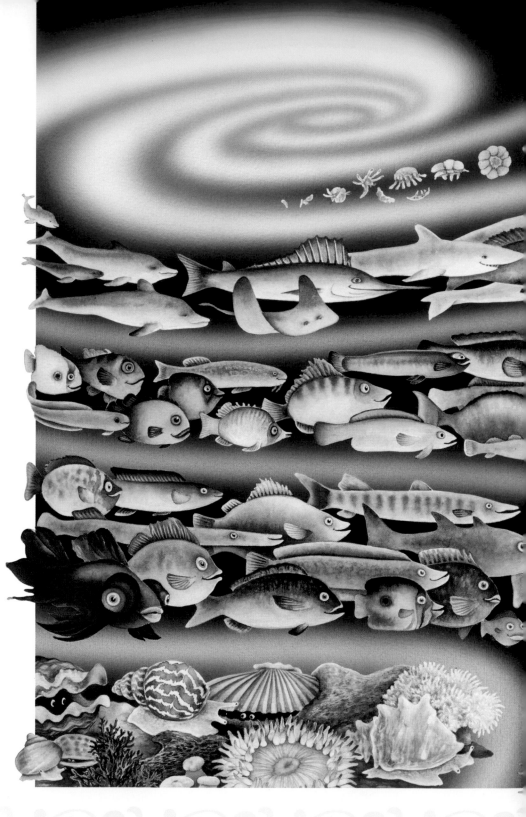

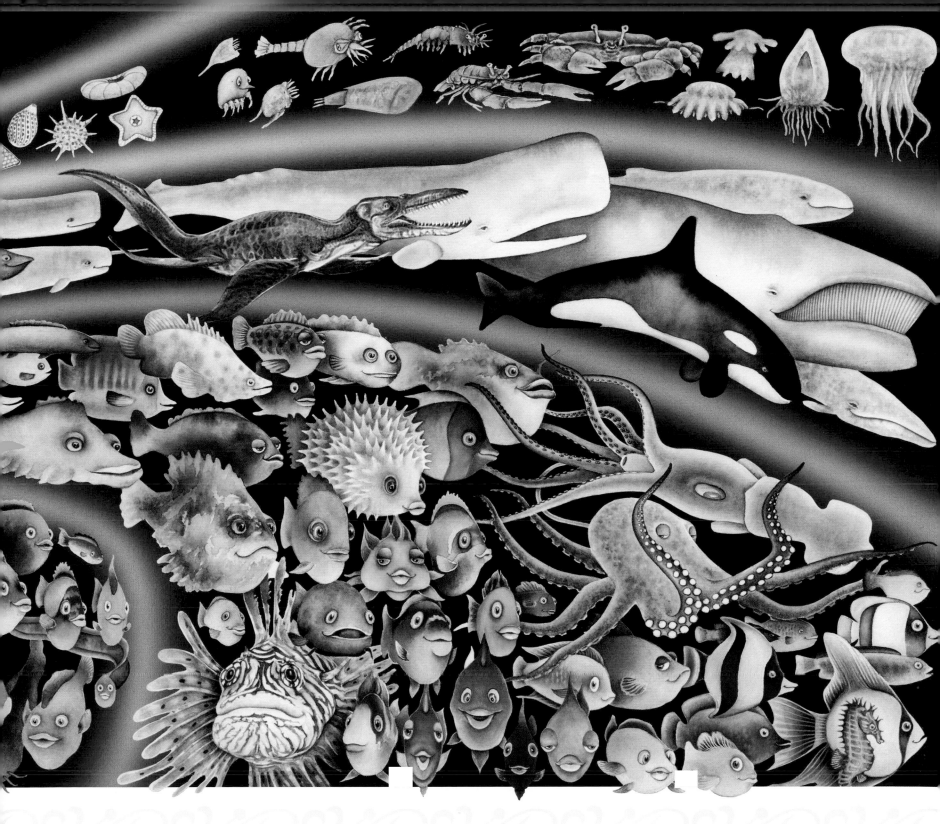

Genesis 1:20–23

"God said...Bring forth abundantly the... fowl that may fly above the earth... And God created...every winged fowl after his kind: and God saw that it was good. And God blessed them, saying, Be fruitful... let fowl multiply in the earth. And the evening and the morning were the fifth day."

God gave birds lightweight, hollow bones so they could fly up high. God also created lots of different wings, beaks, claws, and feathers of every color.

All birds lay eggs, each with their own color and size. God also gave birds their own musical chirps, squawks, and songs for us to enjoy.

Genesis 1:24–25

"And God said, Let the earth bring forth the living creature after his kind, cattle, and creeping thing, and beast of the earth after his kind: and it was so. And God made the beast of the earth after his kind, and cattle after their kind, and every thing that creepeth upon the earth after his kind: and God saw that it was good."

What amazing animals God made! Animals stomp, hop, run, jump, crawl, walk, and swim.

Thousands of different animals and a million kinds of insects roam our earth. Notice their different shapes and colors. Compare their tails, noses, and ears.

Which animals make good pets?

Genesis 1:26, 2:7, 18

"And God said, Let us make man in our image, after our likeness...

The Lord God formed man of the dust of the ground, and breathed into his nostrils the breath of life; and he became a living soul.

And the Lord God said, It is not good that the man should be alone; I will make him an help meet for him."

Now God takes extra time to make a man and a woman. Think of how different people are from all the other creatures.

God gave people the ability to smile and talk, to laugh and cry. We can make and build things. With our big imaginations we can think big thoughts.

Thank You, God, for making all of us people so very special!

Genesis 1:28, 31

"And God blessed [the man and woman], and God said unto them, Be fruitful, and multiply, and replenish the earth, and subdue it: and have dominion over the fish of the sea, and over the fowl of the air, and over every living thing that moveth upon the earth.

And God saw every thing that he had made, and, behold, it was very good. And the evening and the morning were the sixth day."

After creating the man and the woman, God gave them a special blessing. God also told them to have many children.

Then God asked them to take care of the earth and everything in it. How do you help care for fish, birds, and other creatures?

Now God calls *all* of creation "very good." Do you agree?

Genesis 2:2–3

"And on the seventh day God ended his work which he had made; and he rested on the seventh day from all his work which he had made.

And God blessed the seventh day, and sanctified it: because that in it he had rested from all his work..."

Why do you think God made a special day of rest? It wasn't because God felt "tired." Rest is important for all creatures. If we don't take time to rest, what happens? We get grouchy, worn out, and sometimes even sick.

What do you do on your day of "rest?" How can you take time to enjoy God, to enjoy each other, and to enjoy all of CREATION?

The End

God Created Amazing Creatures

Think of all the different sizes, shapes, and colors of the birds, fish, and animals God made. God designed special pouches, arms, legs, eyes, ears, noses, as well as shapes and colors. What an imagination God must have!

An **octopus** has eight long "arms." These arms help an octopus crawl along the sea floor and hang on rocks. The bottom side of each arm is full of suction cups with touch and taste sensors. These sensors help an octopus know if a fish is edible.

A **mouth-brooder fish** takes good care of her eggs. She holds them in her mouth! After the eggs hatch, the mother sometimes blows the baby fish out of her mouth. Then she and her babies have a chance to feed. Then youngsters swim back into mother's mouth at night or in times of danger.

A **father seahorse** is equipped with a special pouch in the front of his body.

The mother seahorse lays up to 400 eggs in his pouch. The father fertilizes the eggs and keeps them warm. When the eggs are ready to hatch, he squeezes his pouch. The babies pop out a few at a time.

The **hummingbird** is the smallest bird God made. Its powerful wings beat 55–75 times a second! Hummingbirds can fly backwards and in every direction, including upside down. They can even hover in one spot like a tiny helicopter.

God gave **bats** a special way to "see" at night. Bats send sonar signals through their nose as they look for food.

These signals bounce off an insect and back to the bat. The bat flies toward the insect by following the returning signals. The bat swallows the insect without having ever seen it.

Each bat knows its own returning signals. Bats never get mixed up with signals from other bats.

Squids swim backwards. They propel themselves by squirting out a strong jet stream of water. When squids are attacked, they change color quickly to startle their enemy, or to blend in with their surroundings. They also squirt out an inky liquid to confuse their attackers.

God Created Amazing Senses

Elephants communicate by touch, smell, and visual signals with their trunk or their flapping ears. Elephants send messages when they trumpet. They also make very low-frequency sounds that cannot be heard by humans. The low sounds travel long distances and help keep the herd together.

The **star-nosed mole** is different from other moles. The end of its nose contains many small tentacles that spread out like a fan. These sensitive tentacles help the mole find insects and worms, even when digging underground In the dark.

An **eagle** needs sharp eyes for hunting.

The eagle's great vision is up to eight times as good as human eyesight.

This keen sense of sight helps an eagle spot fish, rabbits, and gophers while it lies high above the earth.

Sharks have their own electrical detection system. They use it to find their next meal.

Small pores on the underside of the shark's snout pick up another creature's electrical field. This helps the shark locate other fish to eat.

A **snake** uses its tongue to pick up the smell of birds and small animals.

Two tips of the tongue help a snake follow the trail of its prey.

Both forks of the tongue can "taste." More taste on one side means the trail of the prey is turning. Equal taste means the trail goes straight.

Salmon hatch in streams and rivers, then migrate to the sea. After one to four years in the ocean, grown salmon swim hundreds of miles back to the same streams where they were born. They find their way to their home stream by using their keen sense of smell.

Moths use antennae, or feelers, for smelling. Some moths have wide feathered antenna. These feelers pick up smells drifting through the air. This helps the moth track down plants to eat. And it also helps them find other moths.

God Created Amazing Colors and Shapes

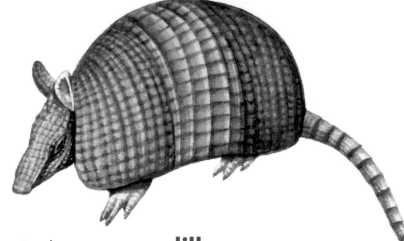

The **Macaw parrot** is the most colorful bird in the world with its bright blue, red, green and yellow feathers.

With its beautiful tail, this parrot grows to be three and a half feet long.

God gave **armadillos** a protective coating like armor. Many hard bands of horny plates protect the armadillo's body. Another tough shield covers and protects the armadillo's head.

When armadillos dig a burrow and hide, they block the entrance with their armor-plated rear so attackers can't enter.

A **hedgehog** rolls up in a tight ball when it feels afraid or when it is threatened by an enemy. Its sharp prickles stick out and protect the hedgehog from attackers.

Some **rabbits** change colors when the seasons change.

In winter, their furry coats turn white and blend in with the snow. This change of color helps the rabbit hide from predators.

The fur coats of **jaguars** and most leopards are covered with spots and speckles.

These spots help jaguars hide easily among small shrubs, ditches, clumps of dry grass, and piles of rocks.

Their spotted coats blend with their surroundings to keep them from being seen when they track and hunt for prey.

Dark patches usually cover the light bodies of **giraffes,** the tallest animals on earth. The brown and white patches on the giraffe's skin blend in with the sunlight and shadows among the trees where they feed.

Velociraptors were dinosaurs that could run very fast. They had a specially-designed claw on their feet to help them in hunting prey. These oversized, sickle-shaped claws were held off the ground while walking.

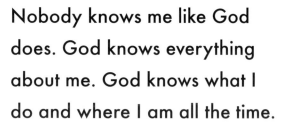

Nobody knows me like God does. God knows everything about me. God knows what I do and where I am all the time.

PSALM 139

PSALM 139:1–3

"O LORD,
thou hast searched me,
and known me.
Thou knowest my downsitting
and mine uprising...
Thou compassest my path
and my lying down, and art
acquainted with all my ways."

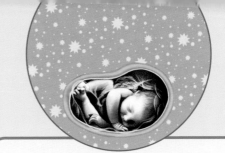

God hears me

Psalm 139:1–2, 4

"O Lord...thou understandest
my thoughts afar off...
For there is not a word in my
tongue, but, lo, O LORD,
thou knowest it altogether."

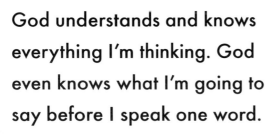

God understands and knows
everything I'm thinking. God
even knows what I'm going to
say before I speak one word.

God is with me

Psalm 139:5, 9, 10

"Thou hast beset me
behind and before, and
laid thine hand upon me...
If I take the wings of
the morning, and dwell in
the uttermost parts of the sea;
Even there shall
thy hand lead me, and
thy right hand shall hold me."

I'm glad I am never alone. God stays close beside me. No matter where I am, God's hand holds me securely.

God formed my body inside my mother. When no one could see me, God saw me and made me.

God formed me

Psalm 139:13, 15

"Thou hast covered me
in my mother's womb...
My substance was not
hid from thee,
when I was made
in secret..."

God made me

Psalm 139:14

"I will praise thee;
for I am fearfully
and wonderfully made:
marvellous are thy works;
and that my soul
knoweth right well."

God made me in an amazing and wonderful way. Even my finger-prints are unique and different.

God numbers my days. Before I lived one minute, God had my whole life written in His book.

God counts my days

Psalm 139:16

"Thine eyes did
see my substance...
and in thy book all my
members were written,
which in continuance were
fashioned, when as yet
there was none of them."

God thinks about me all the time. His thoughts number more than all the grains of sand on every seashore.

God thinks about me

Psalm 139:17–18

"How precious also are
thy thoughts unto me, O God!
How great is the sum of them!
If I should count them,
they are more in number
than the sand…"

God looks into my heart and knows my thoughts. God will lead me in the right way. I will seek God with my whole heart.

God will lead me

Psalm 139:23–24

"Search me, O God,
and know my heart:
try me, and
know my thoughts;
...and lead me
in the way everlasting."

*Thank You, dear God,
For making the world and me.*

New from David and Helen Haidle

Creation-centered activities for active learners from preschool to fourth graders!

Integrated activities develop comprehension and learning skills for first to fourth graders

Suggested teaching schedules are adapted for Christian schools, VBS programs, and homeschoolers

Bible verses form the critical foundation of these structured curriculum lessons

Explains scientific concepts like precipitation, evaporation, types of rocks, clouds, light, and more

Encourages character traits like faith, trustworthiness, thankfulness, and diligence

For the preschooler

God Made the World and Me
8.5 x 11 • Paper • 160 pages
$13.99
ISBN-13: 978-0-89051-563-1

For first to fourth graders

Creation
8.5 x 11 • Paper • 140 pages
$13.99
ISBN-13: 978-0-89051-566-2

Master Books®
A Division of New Leaf Publishing Group
www.masterbooks.net